I0605467

I Like You So Much

To

Why I Like You So Much

From

Date

To my August Ryker, I am a better me because you are you.—Mom

I dedicate this book to all the children who help me see the world as bigger and more colorful, and especially to my daughter Catarina, who brings me the greatest joy in life.—JE

ZONDERKIDZ

I Like You So Much

Zonderkidz, 3950 Sparks Drive SE, Suite 101, Grand Rapids, Michigan 49546

Published in Grand Rapids, Michigan, by Zonderkidz. Zonderkidz is a registered trademark of The Zondervan Corporation, L.L.C., a wholly owned subsidiary of HarperCollins Christian Publishing, Inc.

Requests for information should be addressed to customercare@harpercollins.com.

ISBN 978-0-310-16659-7 (hardcover)
ISBN 978-0-310-16663-4 (audio)
ISBN 978-0-310-16662-7 (ebook)
ISBN 978-0-310-17828-6 (ITPE)

Library of Congress Cataloging-in-Publication Data
Names: Avis, Heather, author. | Eigner, Juliana, illustrator.
Title: I like you so much : a powerful message of celebrating individuality and what makes you unique / Heather Avis ; illustrated by Juliana Eigner.
Description: Grand Rapids, Michigan : Zonderkidz, 2024. | Audience term: Children | Audience: Ages 4-8 | Summary: "This book reminds children that they are likeable just as they are for who they are, exactly as they are-that who they are is enough!"-- Provided by publisher.
Identifiers: LCCN 2024017587 (print) | LCCN 2024017588 (ebook) | ISBN 9780310166597 (hardcover) | ISBN 9780310166627 (ebook)
Subjects: LCSH: Individuality--Juvenile literature. | Developmental disabilities--Juvenile literature. | Love--Juvenile literature. | Self-esteem--Juvenile literature. | CYAC: Individuality. | Love. | Self-esteem. | LCGFT: Picture books.
Classification: LCC BF697 .A95 2024 (print) | LCC BF697 (ebook) | DDC 155.2--dc23/eng/20240913
LC record available at https://lccn.loc.gov/2024017587
LC ebook record available at https://lccn.loc.gov/2024017588

The author is represented by Alive Literary Agency, www.aliveliterary.com.

Zondervan titles may be purchased in bulk for educational, business, fundraising, or sales promotional use. For information, please email SpecialMarkets@Zondervan.com.

Editor: Megan Dobson
Illustrated by: Juliana Eigner
Art direction: Patti Evans
Cover Design: Patti Evans
Interior Design: Mallory Collins

Printed in Johor, Malaysia

25 26 27 28 29 PCA 5 4 3 2 1

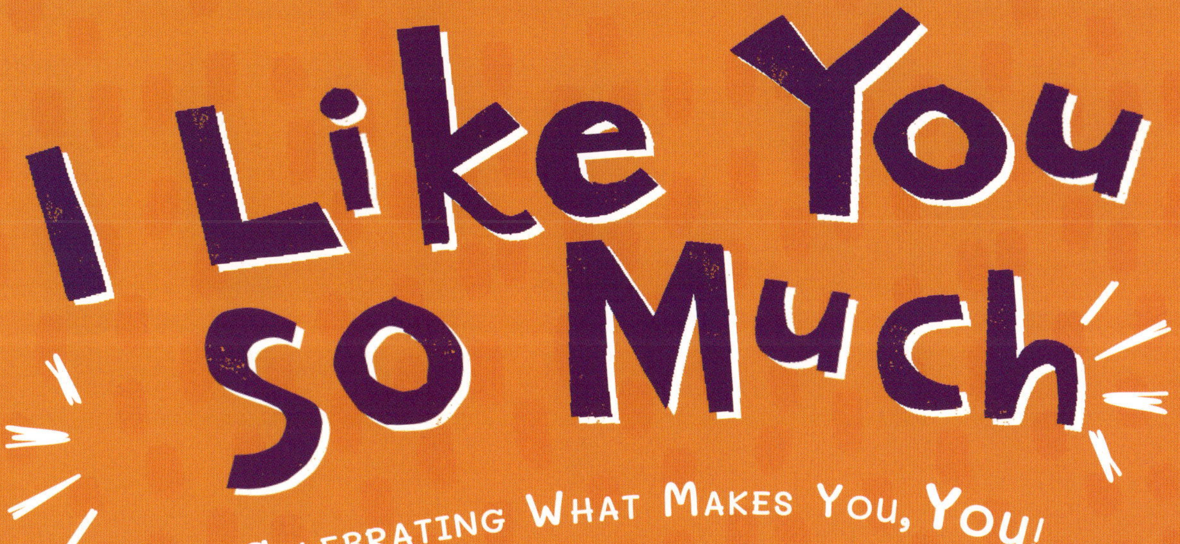

I Like You So Much

Celebrating What Makes You, You!

Heather Avis

Illustrated by
Juliana Eigner

ZONDERkidz

I like you so much.
So, SO, **so much**.
So. Much.
Yes, you!
Oh kid, there is so much to like about you.

Let's start with your face.

I like it so much.

Your face is a stunning,
super-spectacular face.

I like the freckles and spots,
the little birthmarks and the places with
no marks at all.
Your face is the only face like it
in the **whole, wide, wild world.**
I really like your face.

Something else I like about you?

I like the way you feel.

I like when we are side by side and you lean on me and I lean on you and we breathe together at the very same time—in and out!

I like when we snuggle into each other in a big, **humongous, gigantic hug.** You feel so warm and cozy. I like that about you.

I like your entire body.

Just as it is.

I like how there is not another body like yours anywhere in the whole, wide, wild world! I like how you use the body you have to do exactly what your body can do. It's a miracle really, that body of yours.

I like your miraculous brain too!

So much!

I like how amazing your brain is.

I like how it wants to learn and create,
grow and explore.

What a mysterious and wonderful part of you.

I like how your brain helps make you, YOU—
your movements, your thoughts, your sounds.

All of you.

And those sounds of yours—
I really like those too.
I like when you
whistle,
click,
squeak,
or hum.

I like the sound of your excited shriek
when a friend you love comes to play.
And the way you giggle at a funny joke.
All those sounds you make—
I like them so much.

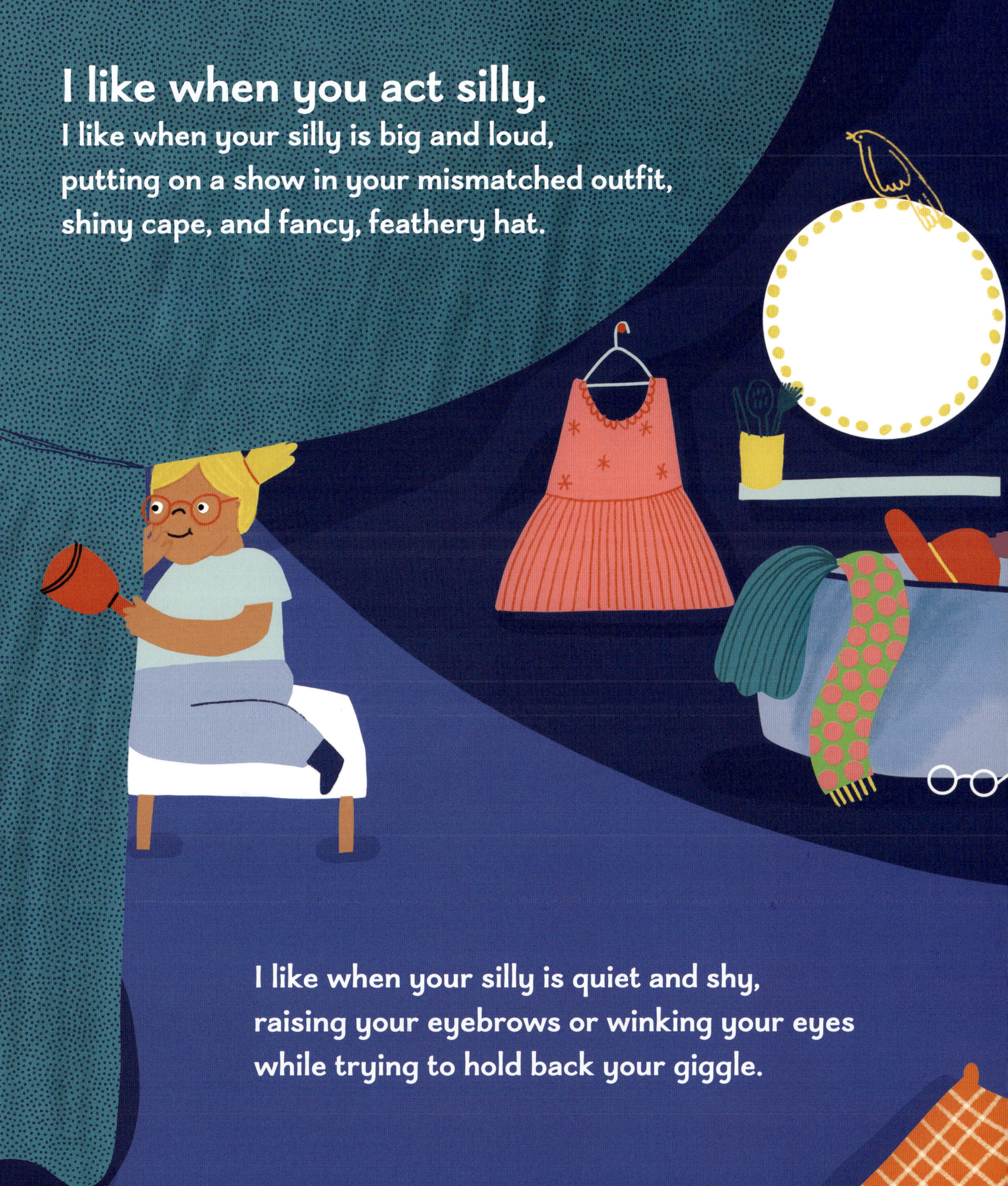

I like when you act silly.

I like when your silly is big and loud,
putting on a show in your mismatched outfit,
shiny cape, and fancy, feathery hat.

I like when your silly is quiet and shy,
raising your eyebrows or winking your eyes
while trying to hold back your giggle.

Sometimes you don't feel silly.
I like that too.
I like how when you feel sad,
you get really quiet and still
and we sit next to each other,
my arm around you.

And you know it's okay to feel sad.

I like how you know that.

You know so much, particularly about people.

I like how that helps you be mindful.

I like how when you come into a room you notice others.
How you just know a classmate is feeling sad or your sisters are feeling afraid.

You're really good at being aware of the people around you and showing them care.
I like that about you.

I like how you love.
Your love is SOOO stretchy.
Stretching from your toys to your dog,
to your family, to your friends—
all the way to yourself.

I like how you love yourself.

How when you see yourself in a mirror
you give a loving, little grin.
You are so good at loving.
I like that about you.

I like how loving yourself means you do your best.

And I like when you do your best.

How sometimes doing your best means a first-place ribbon, and sometimes doing your best means simply showing up.

I like how when you do your best you can celebrate yourself because you know you did your best.

And that's worth celebrating.

You're the best at doing your best.

I like that about you.

Wow!

There is just so much to like **about you!**

Your face . . .

The way you feel . . .

Your body . . .

Your brain . . .

The sounds you make
(especially your giggle) . . .
The ways you are mindful . . .
The ways you love . . .
The ways you do your best . . .

But can you guess the most likable thing about you?

It's you being YOU.

You being you is what this whole, wide, wild world needs the most.

Yes!
YOU

I hope you always know this to be true.
The most likable thing about you is that
you are YOU!

And I hope you like you too!
Because kid—**I like you so much!**

Heather's children Macy, Truly, and August have been her guides in learning to see, celebrate, and embrace our differences. Their lives are a daily reminder of the intrinsic goodness found in all of us . . . just the way we are.

For more from Heather, follow along at @theluckyfewofficial or https://www.heatheravis.com.